Isaac A. Sheppard and Co.

Hints about heating

Containing valuable Suggestions respecting Hot Air Furnace Work

Isaac A. Sheppard and Co.

Hints about heating
Containing valuable Suggestions respecting Hot Air Furnace Work

ISBN/EAN: 9783337208660

Printed in Europe, USA, Canada, Australia, Japan

Cover: Foto ©Suzi / pixelio.de

More available books at **www.hansebooks.com**

HINTS ABOUT HEATING:

CONTAINING

VALUABLE SUGGESTIONS

RESPECTING

HOT AIR FURNACE WORK

TOGETHER WITH

TABLES OF DIMENSIONS, CAPACITIES, ETC.

PREPARED WITH SPECIAL REFERENCE TO THE

Paragon Steel Plate Furnaces

PUBLISHED BY

ISAAC A. SHEPPARD & CO.,

PHILADELPHIA AND BALTIMORE.

Hints About Heating.

Tiis pamphlet is not intended as a manual of information upon the subject of heating by hot air, but simply to point out to purchasers some of the requisites of satisfactory work, and to assist any dealer, who may be without experience in furnace work, to give satisfaction to his customers.

Our climate requires more or less artificial heat during the greater part of the year. If the family is to keep in good health, proper warmth and ventilation in the dwelling are essential; and money spent in securing comfort in these respects will often prevent sickness and save doctors' bills.

Open Fireplaces Insufficient.

OPEN fireplaces are no longer regarded, in this country, as anything more than a pleasant means of supplementing heat derived from other sources. When in actual use, they afford excellent ventilation. For this reason, it is well to provide them in every dwelling. For heating purposes, however, the main reliance must be placed upon either steam or hot water apparatus, or upon Hot Air Furnaces.

Disadvantages of Steam and Hot Water Heating.

STEAM heating, whether direct or indirect, although well adapted to the requirements of large public institutions, is unsuited to ordinary buildings. It is costly; it requires skill and good judgment in its management; it calls for constant attention, and it is expensive to keep in repair. Hot water apparatus, while more safe and more easily managed than steam, is even more costly, and is equally troublesome to keep in repair.

Direct Radiation Unhealthful.

ALL steam or hot water heating, by direct radiation, relies upon heating, over and over again, the air that is *already in the room*. It must certainly be conceded, that such methods of heating are less healthful than one which furnishes a constant supply of fresh, pure air, *taken from the outside atmosphere* and thoroughly warmed before entering the room. This is exactly what is accomplished by a well constructed Hot Air Furnace.

Heating by Warm Air Preferable.

UPON the grounds of superior healthfulness, safety, economy in first cost, ease of management and inexpensiveness of repairs, a good Hot Air Furnace is to be preferred to all other forms of heating apparatus, whenever its use is feasible. No objections have ever been urged against Hot Air Furnaces that cannot easily be shown to originate either in defective construction or in improper management. For the latter, no furnace can justly be blamed. As to the former, it can only be said that furnaces that are defective in construction can always be obtained

4

Hints About Heating.

by those who are unwilling to pay for a good one. On the other hand, it is also true that a good furnace, satisfactorily put up, is within the reach of every person who is willing to pay a fair price. It is to the interest of both the furnace manufacturer and the furnace setter to do their best to satisfy a purchaser who is willing to compensate them reasonably for their outlay.

The Best is the Cheapest.

THIS is a time worn proverb; but it is emphatically true when applied to Hot Air Furnaces. It is an unreasoning and false economy that leads house owners to use a "cheap" type of furnace, put up in a "cheap" way. Good work, in any branch of manufacture, cannot be obtained without paying for it what it is worth. Surely, the health and comfort of one's family are matters of great importance; and those persons who are planning to heat their own homes will not find it to their interest, in the long run, to use poor furnaces improperly set. If they will not pay the furnace man, they may have to pay the doctor.

Even in the case of the houses so often built in our great cities, in long rows, upon speculation, with the intention of selling as quickly as possible, it is to the interest of builders to get good work in this line. Good furnace work will enhance the value of the property, and will help it to an earlier sale, at a better price, than if this important essential were slighted.

It is assumed that those who read these pages want good work, and are willing to pay a reasonable price for it.

5

Furnace Problems of Two Kinds.

THE problems that arise in furnace work are of two kinds, namely:—those that relate to the *production* of heat, and those that relate to its *proper distribution.* The furnace used is responsible *only for the solution of the former*, and even then only when properly managed. The solution of all the problems that relate to the *proper distribution* of the heat supplied by the furnace *rests with the person who sets the furnace.* He decides upon its location, adjusts the hot air pipes and flues, determines upon their sizes, locates the registers and provides for cold air supply. He needs to have not a little good judgment, experience and mechanical skill; for the successful heating of a building depends quite as much upon proper attention to each of these matters as upon the heating capacity of the furnace. Nothing is more common than to find a furnace complained of, when the trouble is entirely due to defects in the mode of distributing the heat produced by it, the arrangements made for this purpose being so insufficient as to make it an impossibility for the hot air generated by the furnace to pass from the furnace to the rooms in which the heat is desired.

Distribution of Heat First Considered.

THE principles that govern the proper distribution of heated air are few; but their application differs more or less in each specific case. Much experience and ingenuity are at times necessary in order to attain the best results. We shall defer, for the present, the discussion of such matters as relate to the pro-

Hints About Heating.

duction of heat, and shall first consider the mode of effecting a *proper distribution* of the warm air generated by a furnace.

Movement of Heated Air.

THREE fundamental facts must be remembered:

    I. Heated air is set in motion *by the pressure of cold air beneath it.*

    II. Heated air always moves most readily *in the direction in which it meets the least resistance.*

    III. The velocity of heated air in a flue *increases* in proportion to the height of the flue and its excess of temperature over that of the outside air.

Upon the observance of these facts all satisfactory hot air heating depends. From the first, we learn the need of a *proper cold air supply.* When the other two are borne in mind, it is apparent that warm air will move more easily in a *vertical* than in a *horizontal* direction, through *short* horizontal pipes more easily than through *long* ones, through *large* pipes more easily than through *small* ones, through *round or square* pipes more easily than through *flat* ones, and more easily through *curved* than through *right angled* elbows. Also, it appears that warm air will move *with the prevailing wind* rather than against it, into a *well ventilated* room rather than into a *close* one, and into an *upper* room in preference to a *lower* one.

The bearing of these well established facts upon the work of intelligent and satisfactory furnace setting, will be seen as the discussion of the subject proceeds.

7

 # Hints About Heating.

Location of Furnace.

THE furnace should always be placed where it will be as easy as possible for the warm air to pass *quickly* and *uniformly* to the rooms that are to be heated by it. Generally speaking, a central position is the most favorable for this purpose; as it causes the lines of pipes to the different hot air flues and registers to be as nearly as possible of *equal length.* This makes the *elevation* of the several pipes as nearly *equal* as possible. Other things being equal, uniformity in distribution is thereby secured. The greater the elevation of a pipe the more easily will the hot air pass through it, and the *shorter* the pipe the *greater its elevation;* so that if a furnace be so placed that some of the pipes are very short and others very long, the short pipes will tend to carry away most of the heat and the long ones will get very little. In cases in which this arrangement cannot be avoided, the short pipes should be made *smaller in size* than the long ones, in order to counteract this tendency.

Heated air always moves slowly and with difficulty through pipes that are horizontal, or nearly so; and hot air pipes should never have an elevation less than 1½ inches per running foot. If the cellar is too low to give such elevation to the pipes, the furnace must be placed in a pit of sufficient depth, lined with brick laid in cement. If the cellar should be damp, the pit should be drained into a drainage well of a greater depth.

That a furnace should be centrally located is not an invariable rule; but it is to be advised in the case of such buildings as are well sheltered from the winter winds. When the exposure of a building is great, as in the case of some corner

8

Hints About Heating.

houses in cities, or of isolated country residences, the furnace should be so placed as to give short runs of pipe to the rooms on the cold side or sides of the building; in other words, to the *north-west of the centre*, so as to secure short runs of pipe to the rooms on the north and north-west. Due provision for the north-east rooms must also be made. In this section of the country the prevailing winds of winter come from the north-west; and the cold, penetrating rain storms from the east and north-east. These winds tend to force the heated air in the building towards the south-east or south-west rooms, necessitating an ample supply to the rooms from which the warm air is liable thus to be driven.

Two or More Furnaces Often Desirable.

In long and narrow buildings, such as the better class of residences in large cities, two furnaces should be used, one to heat the front, and the other the back building. So in general, wherever the use of a single furnace would necessitate a long run of pipe to any part of the building, two or more furnaces are to be advised. A better distribution of heat can always be effected when two furnaces are used, than when only one is employed. An additional advantage in the employment of a second furnace lies in the reserve power thereby afforded in extremely cold weather.

Location of Hot Air Flues and Registers in Dwellings.

Hot air flues should never be placed in an outer wall if it is possible to avoid it. Loss of heat and waste of fuel are

sure to result. When it is impossible to avoid it, a double tin flue should be used in the wall, with a sufficient air space between the inner and outer flues to economize the heat.

Whenever practicable, the flues leading to upper stories should be entirely independent of the first floor supply. The first floor is the floor that it is difficult to heat properly. Having accomplished that to entire satisfaction, little doubt need be felt as to the successful heating of the upper floors.

In locating the registers on the first floor, it is desirable to place them at the most exposed side of the room to be heated, unless to do so should involve a long run of pipe in the cellar. In that case, better results will be obtained by locating the registers so as to get a short run of pipe with a good elevation. Floor registers are the most effective for use on the first floor, as the hot air rises through them with less interference from wind currents, and a more steady flow is obtained than from wall registers. The objections to floor registers are, the necessity of cutting carpets, and the accumulation of dust, sweepings, etc., which can only be avoided by the exercise of great care.

When wall registers are for these reasons preferred, care should be taken to see that they have register boxes of ample size, and that the flow of hot air to and through the register box is *not checked or impeded* by a narrow inlet. Nothing is more common, in city houses, than to find a large wall register set in hall or parlor, with a register box or casing that has an air supply of not more than 3 x 8 inches. Such work cannot be satisfactory. If there is a fireplace in the room, or a ventilating register higher than the hot air register, it is

·Hints About Heating·

well to locate the hot air register on the opposite side, as a better diffusion of heat will thereby be gained before the warm air is withdrawn from the room. Care should be taken, in all cases, not to locate registers where they may interfere with the suitable placing of the furniture of the room.

When these various considerations are comprehended, it is seen how important it is to settle all these matters properly *before the house is built*. It is far more easy and inexpensive to change a *building plan*, than to change a *building*. Architects should make satisfactory heating a primary consideration, and subordinate other details to this.

Hot Air Feed Pipes.

THESE should be of bright charcoal tin, preferably circular in form, either double seamed, or made up with good slip joints lapping not less than 1¼ inches, and well soldered. Sharp turns are to be avoided, and three-piece or four-piece elbows used, where elbows are necessary, in order to diminish friction. Dampers should be placed in each pipe, near the furnace, and marked, by tags or otherwise, to prevent mistakes. For pipes from 10 to 14 inches in diameter, it is desirable to use IX tin. For larger pipes, No. 26 galvanized iron may be used. They should never approach nearer to the joists or ceiling of cellar than 6 inches, and a metal shield should be placed over them when they are nearer than 12 inches.

Vertical Hot Air Pipes.

THESE should be circular in form wherever possible. .While flat or oval pipes are commonly used in walls and partitions, .

such forms increase friction and greatly retard the flow of
warm air; and the area of such pipes should therefore be
correspondingly increased. Brick flues, unless lined with tin
or terra cotta pipe, should not be used for the passage of
hot air. The rough interior of a brick flue impedes the movement of the air; and the absorption of heat by the brick
walls is very great.

Care should be taken to form the "footing piece" or
"starter" of every vertical pipe in such a way as will insure
the quick and easy flow of hot air from the feed pipe into the
vertical pipe; and also to see that the feed pipe is not pushed
into the "footing piece" so far as to cut off any of the supply.
Nothing is more common, in the "cheap" class of furnace
work, than the blunders just indicated.

In some cities, the law requires that where a hot air pipe
is carried up through the centre of a partition, the pipe shall be
double, with ½ inch or more space between the two pipes.
Where this is not required, it is possible by exercising care to
make quite as safe a job by using single pipe. Architects
and builders should be careful so to locate partitions and
studding, that the partition pipe can be carried *straight upward*
throughout its entire length. Offsets tend to accumulate heat
at the points at which they are used, and increase risk of fire
while impeding the flow of heat.

Partition pipe should be kept 3 inches clear of studding
on each side, and the studding protected by a tin lining, for
which purpose the commonest grade of tin may be used. Iron
laths, or coarse screen wire should be used across the pipe
between the studding, in place of wooden lath. To sheathe

Hints About Heating.

the pipe with asbestos felt affords additional protection; and this should be done whenever the pipe approaches sufficiently near the woodwork of flooring or partition to occasion the slightest doubt as to perfect safety.

In old houses, which it is for the first time desired to heat by means of hot air furnaces, and in which the cutting out of partitions is objected to, hot air pipes are often carried to upper rooms through closets on the lower floors. When this is done, the pipes should be well sheathed with asbestos felt, and all exposed woodwork lined with tin.

Another expedient that is sometimes resorted to for heating upper rooms for which no encased hot air flue has been provided, is to carry up a circular pipe *in a corner* of a lower room. This pipe is then concealed from view by studding across this corner at an angle of 45 degrees, nailing iron lath or coarse screen wire across the pipe, between the studding, to receive the plastering, as in the case of a partition pipe. This makes a neat finish, and may be used where the cutting off of the corner is not objected to. The pipe is of course boxed out in the lower room at the proper height from the floor, to receive the register; and, in the upper room, the same finish may be used, or, if preferred, a floor register may be employed, the latter method being the least expensive. By placing a partition in the pipe, and boxing out for an additional register in the adjacent room, it is possible to heat two rooms on each floor by means of the one pipe. The pipe should be reduced in size above the register in lower room, and provided with a hot air damper. Such a pipe should also be sheathed with asbestos felt.

Hints About Heating.

Whenever a hot air pipe passes through a floor or a partition, the woodwork should be cut away for a space of at least 3 inches around the pipe, and protected by a double collar of metal with holes for ventilation, or by the use of a soapstone ring, the latter mode being, in some cities, required by law.

Size of Hot Air Pipes and Registers.

It is not practicable, within the compass of this pamphlet, to lay down rules that shall cover all possible cases. The most elaborate theories often need modification by practical judgment, based upon experience, before they can be satisfactorily applied.

The requirements of the average dwelling, under ordinary conditions, are what are herein referred to.

In determining the size of pipes required, the cubic capacity of the rooms is by no means the only matter to be considered. The *exposure* is of much greater importance. Every square foot of glass, every square foot of exposed wall surface, and every added possibility of the removal of heat by sharp and penetrating winds, increase the demand for hot air supply; and this, of course, means that the size of the pipe used must be proportionately increased. In connection with our Tables of Furnace Capacities, fuller data will be given for the determination of these matters.

Generally speaking, the size of pipes used should be determined with reference to the following considerations:—1. Size of rooms. 2. Exposure. 3. Direction from furnace. 4. Distance from furnace. 5. Height above furnace; *i. e.*, whether on first, second or third floor.

Hints About Heating.

The larger the room, and the greater the exposure, the larger the pipe required. If the direction of the room from the furnace is such that the hot air must·be carried to the room against the prevailing winter winds, the pipe must be *larger* than the pipes used to rooms of like size on the warm side of the house. So also, a room that is at a distance from the furnace must have a larger supply pipe than a room that is near by, in order to make up for the diminished elevation of the pipe.

A room on an upper floor will not require so large a pipe as one of the same size on the first floor; as the greater draft of the vertical pipe increases the velocity, and therefore the quantity, of the hot air passing through it.

As has before been stated, rooms on the first floor are best heated by independent pipes. Rooms on second and third floors can usually be heated satisfactorily by single lines of pipe, reduced in size above second floor register, and furnished with a hot air damper to regulate the flow to the upper room.

Under ordinary conditions, the sizes of pipes and registers indicated below may be recommended:

FIRST FLOOR.

Size of Room in Cubic Feet	Size of Pipe		Size of Register	
	If Round	If Flat	If Round	If Square
Less than 1,500	7 inches	4 x 9 in.	9 inches	7 x 10 in.
1,500 to 2,000	8 "	4 x 12 "	10 "	8 x 10 "
2,000 to 3,000	9 "	4 x 16 "	12 "	8 x 12 "
3,000 to 4,000	10 "	4 x 18 "	12 "	9 x 14 "

, SECOND AND THIRD FLOORS.

USING ONE PIPE, DIMINISHED ABOVE SECOND FLOOR REGISTER.

SIZE OF ROOM IN CUBIC FEET	SIZE OF PIPE TO SECOND FLOOR		SIZE OF DIMINISHED PIPE TO THIRD FLOOR	
	If Round	If Flat	If Round	If Flat
Less than 1,500	8 inches	4 x 12 in.	7 inches	4 x 9 in.
1,500 to 2,000	9 "	4 x 16 "	7 "	4 x 9 "
2,000 to 3,000	10 "	4 x 18 "	8 "	4 x 12 "
	Size of Register—Second Floor		Size of Register—Third Floor	
Less than 1,500	8 x 10 inches		6 x 10 inches	
1,500 to 2,000	8 x 12 "		7 x 10 "	
2,000 to 3,000	9 x 14 "		8 x 10 "	

If the house is but two stories high, use independent pipes to second story rooms, of the sizes indicated in the foregoing tables for diminished pipe to third story rooms, with registers of corresponding size.

In the halls of dwellings, an 8 inch pipe with a 10 inch round or an 8 x 10 inch square register will, in most cases, be found sufficient.

Hints About Heating.

Relative Area of Pipes and Registers.

It should always be remembered that the valves and fretwork of the registers commonly used, reduce their nominal capacity about one-third. The following table of relative areas will be found convenient for reference:—

Hot Air Pipe.		Round Registers		Square Registers	
Size	Effective Area	Size	Effective Area	Size	Effective Area
7 in.	38 sq. in.	7 in.	26 sq. in.	6 x 10 in.	40 sq. in.
8 "	50 "	8 "	33 "	7 x 10 "	46 "
9 "	63 "	9 "	42 "	8 x 10 "	53 "
10 "	78 "	10 "	52 "	8 x 12 "	64 "
11 "	95 "	—	—	9 x 12 "	72 "
12 "	113 "	12 "	75 "	9 x 14 "	84 "
14 "	153 "	14 "	103 "	10 x 12 "	80 "
16 "	201 "	16 "	134 "	10 x 14 "	93 "
18 "	254 "	18 "	169 "	12 x 15 "	120 "
20 "	314 "	20 "	209 "	14 x 18 "	165 "
22 "	380 "	24 "	301 "	16 x 20 "	213 "
24 "	452 "	30 "	471 "	16 x 24 "	256 "

The following table, showing space occupied, opening required, and data from which measurements for tin register boxes may be taken, applies to the Tuttle & Bailey Manufacturing Co.'s registers, sold by us, and may be found useful in getting work ready before arrival of goods. Register boxes should be a trifle larger than dimensions given, and from one to three inches *deeper*, according to size, than the depth of

17

register *when open*. In setting wall registers in shallow flues, as in partitions, the register should be set in a stone border, or else a convex register should be used, so that the flange and valves of the register may not enter into and partially shut off the hot air flue.

DIMENSIONS OF REGISTERS.

TUTTLE & BAILEY MANUFACTURING CO.

Size	Opening to Admit Body of Register	Register Face Outside Measure	Depth of Register		Opening to Admit Iron Border
			Closed	Open	
6 in. Round	6 inches	7¼ inches	1⅝ in.	2½ in.	9½ inches
7 " "	7 "	8⅜ "	1⅞ "	3 "	10⅞ "
8 " "	8⅛ "	9⅜ "	2 "	3⅜ "	12⅜ "
9 " "	9 "	10⅝ "	2¼ "	3⅜ "	13⅜ "
10 " "	10 "	11⅝ "	2⅜ "	3¾ "	14½ "
12 " "	12 "	13¾ "	2⅜ "	3¾ "	16¾ "
14 " "	14⅛ "	15⅝ "	3¼ "	4½ "	18⅞ "
16 " "	16⅛ "	17⅞ "	3½ "	4½ "	21¼ "
18 " "	18 "	19⅞ "	3⅝ "	5 "	23⅝ "
20 " "	21⅞ "	21⅞ "	4 "	5⅝ "	24⅝ "
24 " "	24¼ "	26½ "	4¾ "	6½ "	32 "
30 " "	30 "	32 "	4¾ "	6½ "	37¼ "
6 x 10 in. Sq.	6⅛ x 10 in.	7⅞ x 12 in.	1⅞ "	2¼ "	10½ x 14¾ in.
7 x 10 "	7 x 10 "	8¾ x 11¾ "	2 "	2¾ "	11⅞ x 14⅞ "
8 x 10 "	8 x 10 "	9⅝ x 11⅝ "	2 "	3 "	13⅛ x 15 "
8 x 12 "	8 x 12 "	9¾ x 13⅝ "	2 "	3 "	12¾ x 16½ "
9 x 12 "	9⅛ x 12⅛ "	10¾ x 13¾ "	2¼ "	3⅜ "	14⅛ x 17 "
9 x 14 "	9⅛ x 14 "	11 x 16 "	2¼ "	3⅜ "	14 x 19⅛ "
10 x 12 "	10 x 12 "	11⅞ x 13⅞ "	2⅜ "	3⅝ "	15 x 17 "
10 x 14 "	10 x 14 "	12¼ x 16⅛ "	2⅜ "	3⅝ "	15½ x 19½ "
12 x 15 "	12 x 15⅛ "	13⅝ x 16⅞ "	2¾ "	4¼ "	16½ x 19¾ "
14 x 18 "	14⅛ x 18⅛ "	16½ x 20¼ "	2⅝ "	3⅞ "	20⅛ x 23¾ "
16 x 20 "	16 x 20⅜ "	17⅝ x 22⅛ "	3 "	4½ "	21⅛ x 25⅝ "
16 x 24 "	16⅛ x 24⅜ "	18⅛ x 27 "	3 "	4½ "	21⅞ x 30½ "

Hints About Heating.

Churches, Stores and Public Buildings.

THESE structures present somewhat different conditions from those that are encountered in dwelling houses. All that has been said as to the underlying principles of warm air heating of course holds good; but their application is modified by the circumstances of each case. Systematic and well planned ventilating arrangements are much more frequently found in these buildings than in ordinary dwellings. These serve to facilitate the heating of a building; but they also call for larger heating capacity in the furnaces selected. The mistakes usually made in such cases, are the selection of furnaces that are too small, and the endeavor to make one furnace do the work of two.

In locating registers for church heating, the endeavor should be to distribute the heat *evenly* throughout the building. A register should always be placed *near each entrance*, in order that the effect of the influx of cold air, consequent upon the frequent opening of the doors, may be counteracted. Other registers should be placed wherever they are necessary to carry the heat equally to all parts of the room.

The location of registers having first been determined, the next thing to ascertain is whether these registers can be reached by short runs of pipe, with a good elevation, *from a single furnace*. If not, it may be regarded as settled that more than one furnace will be required.

Try groups of three or four registers, and see whether a point can be found that will give nearly equal, and moderately short, runs of pipe to the registers of each group, and

locate furnaces accordingly. Having found the number of furnaces necessary, it will be easy to determine upon their proper size and capacity.

Never locate a register immediately over a furnace. It is a source of discomfort, to those who sit near it, by reason of the intense heat and strong draft arising from it; while the heat rises rapidly to the ceiling without dispersing its benefits to those who are a little further removed from it. Two or three registers of a smaller size, each located eight or ten feet away from the furnace, will give far more pleasant and satisfactory results.

In arranging the registers for a store, care should be taken to place one *near the entrance*. The location of the others should depend upon the ordinary uses of certain parts of the building. Where sorting, handling and packing of goods is usual, less heat will be needed than in those parts of the building in which persons are engaged in sedentary occupation. In stores in which skylight openings are cut through to the first floor, the first floor registers should be so placed as to prevent the warm air from rising through the opening until after its heat has been well diffused throughout the first floor.

Cold Air Supply.

THIS should never be taken from the cellar if it is possible to avoid doing so; but it should be brought from the outer air, by means of a cold air duct, which may be constructed of brick, galvanized iron or wood, as may be preferred. The sectional area of this duct should be not less than three-fourths

Hints About Heating.

of the sectional area of all the hot air pipes leading from the furnace. Thus if four 9 inch pipes are to be supplied with warm air, their total area being 252 square inches, the cold air duct should measure 10 x 19 inches inside, or its equivalent. If one cold air opening in the base of the furnace is inadequate to receive this supply, the duct should be divided into two parts, and one carried to an opening on each side of the furnace base.

Whenever possible, take the cold air from either the north or the west side of the building, as it is from the north-west that the prevailing cold winds of winter come. Put a slide in the cold air duct, arranged so that it can be closed one-half, should an unusual wind-pressure render it necessary, but so that it can never be entirely shut off. The outer opening of the duct should be closed by a wire screen, to prevent the entrance of animals. When a settling chamber and filtration apparatus can be provided, all dust may be removed from the air before its admission to the furnace; but, except in the best jobs of work, the expense of such an appliance occasions objection. Very excellent work can be done if cost is a secondary consideration.

The best method of introducing the cold air to the furnace is *from beneath*. This involves the use of a furnace with closed base and sides, and an open bottom. Place the furnace over a pit, lined with brick laid in cement, first building a central pier up to the ash pit, to support the weight of the furnace. The cold air duct should be so connected with this pit as to secure a perfectly uniform distribution of the cold air around the furnace, in order that the diffusion of heat from

Hints About Heating.

the radiating surfaces may be rapid and uniform. When it is not desired to incur this expense, a furnace with closed bottom may be used, and the cold air introduced thereto by means of suitable collars in the sides of the casing.

If it is impracticable to get a direct cold air supply, and the air has therefore to be taken from the cellar, the cellar must be kept perfectly clean, and as free from dust as possible; and an inlet for fresh air must be provided by carrying a pipe of the proper size from a window, or an opening in the wall, to a point within twelve or fourteen inches of the cellar floor. The cold air so introduced will flow in a direct line to the furnace, without creating an unpleasant draft in the cellar. Such an expedient, however, should not be resorted to if there is any way of reaching the furnace by a regular cold air duct.

If there are any turns or bends in the cold air duct, care should be taken to avoid any diminution of its area at such points. It must be of *full size throughout*. A furnace cannot supply warm air unless it is first fed with the air that it is expected to heat.

When a public hall or the audience room of a church is to be heated by a hot air furnace, it is sometimes advantageous to make a connection between the cold air duct of the furnace and the room to be heated, arranging it so that this connecting pipe may be entirely closed by a slide. Until the room is occupied by the audience, the cold air may thus be drawn from the room itself and returned to it warmed, the heating process then going on rapidly. As soon as the audience begins to assemble, the connecting pipe from the

22

·Hints About Heating.

room should be closed, and the outer cold air supply opened; so that thereafter a supply of pure warm air will be furnished to the room, already comfortably heated.

When it is desired to place a furnace in the basement of a church or other building, and to heat the basement as well as the upper part of the building thereby, the cold air supply should be carried to the furnace beneath the basement floor. To obtain good results, the furnace should be fitted with but a single casing, which should be of Russia iron, in order that the heat may be freely radiated into the basement room. An upper door or doors should be placed in the casing, and a damper in each of the hot air pipes that lead to the room above. The entire heat of the furnace may then, if desired, be retained in the basement by closing the hot air dampers and opening the upper door. or doors of the furnace.

Ventilation.

IN order to remove the carbonic acid gas and organic impurities produced by respiration, and to make good the constant withdrawal of oxygen by the burning of lights at night, some provision for a continual change of the air of inhabited rooms is necessary. This ventilation it is the province of the architect to arrange for; and the furnace setter is rarely consulted. The latter has in most cases to be content with such ventilation as he finds to have been already provided when his own work begins. Yet unless some way is at hand whereby the air that is already in a room may flow out, it is manifest that the hot air which the furnace is ready to supply cannot flow

into it. Sometimes the quickest way to heat a room is to lower a window slightly, to give the cold air in a room a chance to escape freely, and make room for the admission of the warm air that would otherwise enter but slowly.

To discuss the subject of ventilation at length would require a volume. Only a passing notice, rendered necessary by the intimate connection of ventilation and heating, is possible here.

The use of open fireplaces, as has before been said, so long as fire is kept in them, furnishes to many dwellings a good method of ventilation. When the fire is out, a down draft often occurs in the chimney, which renders it useless as means of removing vitiated air. In large buildings, such as churches and halls, systematic provision is usually made for ventilation; but many dwellings are without suitable arrangements of this sort. The most common method of ventilating dwellings is that of employing outlet flues, which are kept warm either by being built in immediate contact with the smoke flues of the furnace and of the kitchen range, or by having the smoke pipes carried up through the ventilating flues, using for the purpose a pipe made either of cast or wrought iron, or terra cotta. The warmth thus obtained creates an upward current in the ventilating flues, and the vitiated air is drawn out of the rooms and up the flues through registers suitably located and opening into the ventilating flues, either directly or through ventilating pipes.

Some persons argue that ventilating registers should be placed near the floor of the room. They base this opinion upon the fact that carbonic acid gas, *when unmixed*, is heavier

than common air at the same temperature; and they therefore contend that, as it is produced in a room by respiration, it will fall to the floor, and that it can be removed only by means of outlets at the floor. This notion fails to take into account the law of transfusion of gases, which teaches us that at the moment carbonic acid gas is exhaled from the lungs, it at once intermingles with the air throughout the entire room. It also overlooks the fact that, when it passes out of the lungs, the human breath, loaded with organic impurities as well as with carbonic acid gas, is at the bodily temperature of 98 degrees, while the ordinary temperature of a properly heated room is only about 70 degrees. The heated breath, therefore, rises at once to a level that corresponds with its temperature; so that the foulest air in a room will ordinarily be found at a higher level than the heads of its occupants. If any one doubts this, let him simply stand upon a table in a heated room of ordinary height, and find whether the air that he will then inhale is purer and sweeter than the air he was breathing when he stood upon the floor.

Observation leads to the belief that in ordinary dwellings the most satisfactory results are attained when the ventilating registers are placed near the ceiling. This plan, of course, continually withdraws heat from the room, and demands an ample supply of hot air, larger furnaces and more fuel. Like almost every other good thing, good ventilation costs money. When economy of fuel is an object, place the ventilating registers near the floor. Architects often provide outlet registers near the floor and near the ceiling also, leaving the occupants of the house free to open either at their pleasure.

We repeat that wherever means of artificial ventilation have been provided, the furnace should be of ample capacity, otherwise the rooms may be cold when the ventilating registers are open; and if they are not to be opened, they might as well not exist at all.

Fortunately in ordinary dwellings, tenanted, as most of our American homes are, by but a few persons, natural ventilation furnishes all the change of air that is indispensable to health, if the rooms are heated by a good hot air furnace, well supplied by cold air from without. The pure warm air that enters the room from the furnace is *constantly displacing an equal amount* of the air that was previously in the room. If this were not so, the warm air could not enter the room at all.

This displacement is made possible by the outlet that is afforded by crevices in floors and around window frames, and by loosely fitted doors and window sashes, and lastly, though not least, by diffusion through the walls themselves. This has been shown, by Pettenkofer's experiments, to be not less than seven cubic feet of air per hour for each square yard of wall surface (brick wall, plastered, but not papered), when the difference between the temperature within and without is 40 degrees. In a room 12 x 15 x 10 feet, this diffusion would amount to 2800 cubic feet per hour.

As has before been said, ordinary dwellings are large in proportion to the number of persons who live in them; and natural ventilation is often adequate to effect the necessary change of air. In the light of what has been said, however, the great importance of a plentiful supply of pure air to the

Hints About Heating.

furnace must clearly appear, and also the fact that it is short sighted economy to stint the size of the furnace used. No matter whether reliance is placed upon natural or artificial ventilation, *ample furnace power* must be provided if a steady and adequate change of air in the rooms is to be secured.

Supply of Moisture.

THIS is a matter of some importance. As air is heated, its capacity for absorbing moisture proportionately increases. If there be no arrangement made for supplying this moisture directly to the air as it is heated, it will be drawn from the wood work and furniture in the house, causing annoying and damaging cracks and shrinkage. The health of the occupants of the room also will suffer, as the needed moisture will be taken up by the heated air from the bodily surfaces and the mucous membranes, thereby rendering the persons susceptible to cold, and occasioning many catarrhal troubles. In all our furnaces provision is made for a water supply; and the pans provided for that purpose should always be kept filled with water.

Production of Heat.

HAVING thus briefly referred to the problems that are properly grouped under the distribution of heated air, the problems involved in the generation of heat remain to be considered. These consist of matters that relate to furnace *connections*, furnace *construction*, and furnace *management*. Under the head of furnace connections, the smoke pipe and chimney demand attention.

Smoke Pipe.

THIS is best made of heavy galvanized iron, well riveted, each section entering the next by a lap of not less than one and one-half inches. The size should be the same throughout as that of the pipe collar of the furnace, and it should run as directly as possible from furnace to chimney, with a steady ascent all the way. Where turns in the pipe are unavoidable, three-piece or four-piece elbows should be used. If the pipe is long and the cellar cold, it will be well to wrap the pipe with asbestos sheathing to prevent loss of heat, which results in impaired draft.

It is well to rivet a flange or collar to the pipe some five inches from the end that enters the chimney. This will prevent the pipe from being pushed at any time too far into the chimney, and will also serve to prevent the leakage of air into the chimney around the pipe. The pipe hole in chimney should be made to fit the pipe neatly. The pipe should be securely wired to the chimney to prevent displacement, and supported throughout its entire length by strong wiring to joists at proper intervals. Screw hooks are better to wire to than nails, and make a neater finish.

If the smoke pipe has to pass through any partitions, double collars of metal should be used around it with a space of three or four inches between them, this space being ventilated by ample perforations. The pipe should be kept as far as possible from any exposed wood work, and the wood work protected by asbestos sheathing or bright tin, or both, according to the relative position and nearness of the pipe.

Hints About Heating.

Chimney.

THE chimney with which a furnace is connected is a matter of great importance. "Draft," as it is called, is a function of the *chimney*, not of the furnace. The upward movement of air in the chimney is due to the difference in weight between the warm air in the chimney and the cold air outside. The more nearly equal the temperature within and without the chimney shaft, the weaker the "draft;" and, *vice versa*, the greater the difference of temperature the stronger the draft. The longer the column of air in the chimney, the stronger will be the draft; so that, other things being equal, the taller the chimney, the more powerful will be the movement of heated air within it. Leakage of air into the shaft at any point diminishes the upward pressure; and if the inside is rough, the draft will be impeded by the friction of the chimney walls.

Poor chimneys occasion much trouble; and the difficulties that are due to their imperfect construction are often the source of complaints respecting the operation of furnaces. Chimneys should always be built in the *inner walls* of houses, where possible. If they must be built in exposed outer walls, let the wall selected be a south or east wall, and not one on the north or west side. The chimney should be of adequate size for the work required of it, but *not too large*. For ordinary purposes, a round flue of smooth terra cotta or tile, of 8 inches inside diameter, is the best. A flue 8 x 8 or 8 x 12 inches in the clear, smoothly pargetted with good mortar, however, will be found to give good results, if of proper height.

Hints About Heating.

Chimneys should, if possible, be topped out *above the highest point* of the roof of the building, in order that the wind, in passing over the roof, may not occasion downward currents in the flues and impair or destroy the draft. A clean-out door should always be located at the base of the chimney; and the bricklayer should always leave the chimney clear of any mortar or other debris.

If hot air flues are built in chimney adjoining the smoke flue, they should be well lined with tin, and the intervening wall well built and carefully pargetted to prevent leakage of gas into the hot air flues.

Before connecting a furnace with the chimney, the chimney should be carefully examined, and cleared of all accumulations of soot or other obstructions, any cracks in chimney stopped, and all unused pipe holes tightly closed.

A Few Words About Gas.

IT should always be remembered that it is upon *the condition of smoke pipe and chimney* that freedom from gas depends. Combustion generates gases that will find their way out from the furnace by the channel that offers the *least resistance.* If the draft of the chimney is good and the smoke pipe unobstructed, they will readily pass out into the chimney. Under such conditions, the air pressure upon the furnace is *from without, inwards;* and even if there should be any defects in the joints of the furnace, (a thing which after long use may possibly occur), air will be carried, through such a defective joint, *into* the furnace, instead of gas passing out through it.

Hints About Heating.

If, however, the outlet into the chimney be so impeded, or the draft of the chimney so defective, that the gas finds *less resistance* in passing out through the joints of the furnace than through the smoke pipe and chimney, it will seek an outlet through the joints into the hot air chamber; or, if the furnace joints are absolutely gas tight, it will pass into the cellar through the doors of the furnace. A good flue, ample connections and a steady fire, afford the surest guarantee of freedom from gaseous products.

Furnace Construction.

A WELL constructed furnace is one that combines simplicity and ease of management with durability, freedom from gas and dust, and large radiating surface in proportion to the area of the surface of the grate. These essentials having been first secured, compactness of form and economy of first cost are to be sought for. We know of no other Portable Furnace that so fully meets all these requirements as the PARAGON FURNACE, and next to it, the FIDELITY; although we also make other excellent goods of this sort, which maintain a deserved popularity. This part of the subject will be further considered in connection with the description of each furnace.

Furnace Management.

SPECIFIC directions for the successful use of particular furnaces will be given in their proper place. Some general instructions, applicable to all alike, may be given in a few words.

The coal used should be of good quality, and *not too large*. The proper sizes of anthracite coal are a *medium stove size*, for furnaces of moderate capacity, and *large stove size*, or "*egg*" coal, for furnaces with 40 inch casing and upwards. The so called "white ash" coals give more heat than the "red ash," but require a stronger draft for complete combustion. Where the draft is good, the "white ash" coal is to be preferred.

The fire chamber *must be kept clear*, any accumulations of ashes or clinker being removed as fast as they form. Ashes and clinker have *no heating power*.

"No heat without fuel." The fire chamber *must be kept full* if the house is to be kept warm. A few inches depth of coal upon the grate is insufficient.

A *moderate but steady fire* should be kept. Less clinker will be produced, less wear upon the furnace occasioned, and less coal consumed than by alternately letting the fire burn violently, and then suddenly checking it. Irregular firing burns out furnaces and wastes fuel.

After fresh coal is put on the fire, it should always *be allowed to burn up a little* until the fresh coal is heated through. This prevents the chilling of the fire and causes the gas that arises from the fresh fuel to pass freely into the chimney.

Ashes should be entirely removed from the ash pit at least *once in every twenty-four hours*. Ashes left under the grate impair the draft of the furnace, and *cause the grate to burn out*. It is cheaper to attend to this than to buy new grates.

Hints About Heating.

Carefully study the varying draft of the flue with which the furnace is connected, and regulate the furnace in the way which experience demonstrates is best suited to the conditions under which it operates. These differ in almost every case, and can be determined only by close observation.

If the house is to be comfortable in the morning, the furnace must be so regulated in the evening as to keep the temperature of the lower rooms from falling too low during the night.

Intelligence, observation and patience are necessary to manage properly any form of heating apparatus. The exercise of these qualities sometimes fails in the case of servants, to whom the management of furnaces is ordinarily entrusted. In such instances some member of the family should supplement the deficiencies of the person who has the care of the furnace.

Importance of Proper Plans.

WHAT has been said respecting the location of hot air flues and registers, emphasizes the importance of planning suitable arrangements for the house-heating *before the house is erected*. It is not only unfair to the furnace setter, but a detriment for all time to the occupants of the house, to build it without carefully arranged and suitable provision for a proper distribution of hot air throughout the dwelling. Many an architect, sound as his professional judgment may be regarding most matters, would find it of great advantage to submit his plans for hot air work to a skilled and intelligent furnaceman

33

before their completion. He will then find that when the time comes to set the furnace in place, it will not be necessary either to put up with unsatisfactory results or to make expensive and annoying alterations in the building.

In cases in which it is the intention to specify furnaces of our manufacture in new buildings, we shall be glad, so far as our engagements will permit, to confer with architects or builders respecting these matters, and to make any suggestion that may aid them in obtaining the best results.

False Economy.

A WORD of caution here to owners of property :

There are all sorts and sizes of furnaces, and all sorts and kinds of furnace work. The poorest is cheap enough. That which is really good cannot be had without paying for it what it is worth. The man who flatters himself that he is getting *more than what he pays for* is grievously mistaken. If the work of setting a furnace is slighted, the furnace will be overtaxed, and it will soon burn out. So also, if the furnace be of poor quality, or if it be too small to do the work required of it, it will not last long, and a new one will soon have to be purchased. Meanwhile, the occupants of the building will be more or less inconvenienced, and perhaps injured in health. Such attempted saving is *false economy*. To buy a furnace of good quality and of ample capacity, and to have all the work connected with it properly arranged and put up of good material, in a thoroughly workmanlike manner, will be found the most satisfactory, as well as the cheapest plan, in the end.

Hints About Heating.

What We Need to Know.

WHEN we are asked for information or advice respecting furnace work, or the selection of a furnace, the following information should be given us:—

I. Is the building constructed of brick, stone or wood?

II. Is it one of a block, or does it stand alone?

III. If alone, is it much exposed? Give particulars.

IV. Draw a plan, no matter how rough, of the cellar and of each floor above. Mark dimensions of each room. State height of ceilings of each story; and the height of cellar clear of joists. Mark location and size of smoke flues and of hot air flues; also any open fireplaces, and any closets or recesses through which hot air pipes may be run if necessary. Mark also the location preferred for each register.

V. Mark the points of the compass on the plan.

VI. If any girders in cellar, mark them on plan and state their clear height above cellar floor. Mark also any piers or other obstructions to the run of hot air pipes in cellar.

VII. State whether there are any objections or difficulties to interfere with digging a pit in cellar to lower the furnace, if necessary to do so, in order to give a better elevation to the hot air pipes.

Hints About Heating.

VIII. Mark on plan the cellar window or other opening through which the cold air supply is to be taken. Remember that this should be on north or west side of building.

IX. If a church or other public building, mark on plan the location of doors, windows, vestibules, aisles, pulpit, etc., also ventilating flues, if any. Also state whether there are any open spaces under pews for circulation of air.

X. State whether the building is still to be constructed, or whether it has already been completed.

NOTE.—If the building has not yet been erected, the details of heating plan should be settled without delay, in order that suitable provision for a good job of work may be made as the structure is built. Proper plans insure the comfort of the occupants, as well as economy of fuel and durability of heating apparatus.

Hints About Heating.

The Paragon Steel Plate Furnace, with Equalized Draft.

Patented, August 5th, 1890.

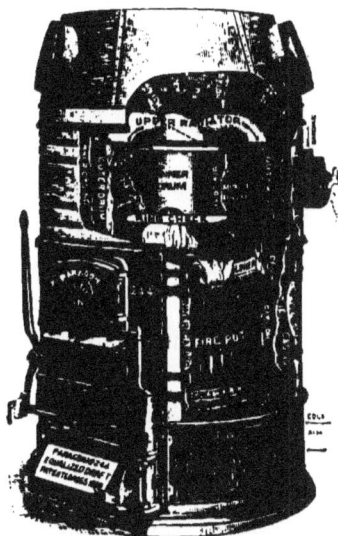

THE construction of this furnace embodies the latest and most desirable improvements that modern ingenuity has suggested. Since the patent upon this construction, embracing five distinct specifications, was granted to us, the PARAGON FURNACE has attracted an unusual amount of attention and attained a conspicuous success.

Its characteristic features will be seen by examining the engravings upon the pages that follow.

Upon a strong and roomy ash pit is placed a heavy, corrugated fire pot, the joint being arranged to pack with sand and cement, to make it perfectly gas tight. The fire pot is surmounted by a heavy casting known as the lower radiator, which is cast in one piece. This is carefully proportioned in thickness, and strengthened throughout by corrugation, to prevent cracking by fire. The joint between the lower radiator and the fire pot is also a sand joint.

Three heavy steel plate drum-casings are accurately fitted to flanges cast upon the upper surface of the lower radiator. The upper edges of these drum-casings are securely adjusted to the flanges of an upper radiator, which, like the lower radiator, is cast in one piece.

The inner drum casing forms a central smoke chamber, an outer smoke chamber being afforded by the space between the middle and the outer drum casing. These two smoke chambers *communicate freely with each other and with the fire pot*, and are *perfectly self-cleaning*. The passage of the draft through them is carefully regulated by self-cleaning checks, so proportioned as to obtain a perfectly *equalized draft* and a uniform distribution of heat over the entire radiating surface of the drums.

Between the central and the outer smoke chamber is an annular hot air space, to which the air to be heated passes freely through inclined passages formed in the lower radiator.

The feed door neck is cast in one piece with the lower radiator, and also communicates with the outer smoke chamber, whereby any possibility of flame being blown out through the feed door is avoided.

The base section is made in two forms, octagonal and round. Cold air may be introduced at the sides, back, or from beneath the furnace, at pleasure. The cold air openings in the base are provided with removable panels, which may be either open or close, as ordered. The ash pit door is so arranged that the draft may be regulated by either a ratchet or a chain.

Points of Advantage.

THE essential points of advantage that are possessed by the PARAGON over all other three drum furnaces, are as follows:

    I. The inner and outer combustion chambers communicate with each other in such a way that *all the radiating surfaces* of both combustion chambers *are equally heated.*

Hints About Heating.

II. Both combustion chambers are *absolutely self-cleaning*.

III. Both the upper and lower radiator castings are *made in one piece*, so that there are *no joints* between cast iron surfaces above the fire pot level.

We do not need to say to experienced furnace setters that there is *no other three-drum furnace made* that embraces the three points above named in its construction. It has long been conceded that a perfect three-drum furnace must possess these requisites; but until the problem was solved in the PARAGON FURNACE, manufacturers thought that it was a practical impossibility to combine them. The successful accomplishment of this feat has placed the PARAGON at the head of all furnaces of this class. Its most conspicuous merits are enumerated in the pages that follow.

Great Radiating Power.

THE PARAGON FURNACE possesses the *largest radiating surface*, in proportion to grate surface, of any three-drum furnace yet made. The equalized draft renders every square inch of this surface *equally effective*. The result is three fold:—an ample and constant supply of warm air; an *equal wear* upon all parts of the furnace; and perfect utilization of the heat of the fuel. This means *superior economy, efficiency* and *durability*.

No Heat Lost in Cellar.

THE PARAGON FURNACE is *double cased throughout*, the air space between the casings serving as a non-conducting chamber, preventing loss of heat and increasing the efficiency of the furnace. What is desired is to heat the *house*, and *not the cellar*. This the PARAGON accomplishes.

39

Hints About Heating.

Effective Ventilation Secured.

THE ample provision made in the structure of the PARAGON for the admission of air, and for its rapid distribution in large volumes over the heating surfaces, insures adequate ventilation. It brings about a constant influx of pure warm air into the rooms to be heated, which continually displaces an equal amount of vitiated air, and establishes the claim of the PARAGON to be regarded as an effective ventilating apparatus.

No Dry, Parched Air, but Pleasant Warmth.

A LARGE water pan is provided at the front of the furnace, just where it can most easily be examined and most conveniently filled. Constant evaporation from the surface of the water contained therein furnishes the needed moisture. The water pan is protected from undue heat by interposing the dust flue between it and the fire pot; while the liability of the fire pot to burn out in front, where very little air comes into contact with it, is diminished by placing the water pan at that point.

Perfect Combustion.

THE construction of the PARAGON FURNACE, although so simple that it can be understood by a child, is nevertheless unsurpassed in securing perfect combustion. The draft is always *direct*, and perfectly *equalized* throughout. The fire can be kindled in about half the time required by other three-drum furnaces. The combustion will be found *perfectly equal* throughout the whole mass of fuel. This results in comparative freedom from clinker, and in thorough utilization of

the fuel. A large amount of heat—a small residue of ashes and clinker—these are the results attained by the PARAGON FURNACE.

Ease of Management.

THE draft is regulated by raising or lowering the drop shutter in the ash pit door, and by closing or opening the draft check at the back of the furnace. Both of these are held at any desired point by means of a ratchet; or if preferred, they may be connected with a chain, and thereby operated from the room above. In the ROUND BASE PARAGON, which is supplied with the draw centre grate, the whole surface of the grate is exposed to view upon opening the sliding fire doors. By means of the poker, clinker can be easily removed from any part of the fire, and dropped through the centre of grate into the ash pit. The grate is hung upon frictionless bearings, and connected with a lever shaker. A person can operate this without stooping; and its action is so easy that a child can thoroughly shake the grate of the largest furnace. In the OCTAGON BASE PARAGON, the purchaser has the choice also of the famous ''Triplex Grate,'' which has many zealous advocates, or of the ''Saxon Grate,'' which many think has no superior.

Superior Cleanliness.

THE ash pit of the PARAGON is capacious, and the ash pit door both wide and deep, affording every facility for the easy removal of ashes. A dust flue, placed *at the front* where it is needed, (not at the back of the ash pit where

41

·Hints About Heating·

it is liable soon to be choked up with refuse, and rendered useless), protects the operator from annoyance. As has before been said, the drums are self-cleaning throughout, and require no attention.

Freedom from Gas.

THE PARAGON FURNACE is in this respect faultless. Its superiority in construction will be manifest to any one who will examine competing furnaces. In the PARAGON FURNACE the lower radiator, (sometimes called the "crab,") is *made in one piece*,—absolutely *jointless*.

In all other furnaces of this class, this "crab" is usually made in *three parts*, never in less than *two*. These parts, owing to their peculiar formation, expand and contract irregularly, becoming warped and distorted, and opening the joints between them at the very points at which gas and smoke are most liable to escape into the hot air chamber. No matter how carefully made and tightly cemented these joints at first may be, it is absolutely impossible to keep them tight in actual use. In such constructions, leakage of gas is *unavoidable*. In the PARAGON lower radiator, it is *impossible*.

The upper radiator of the PARAGON is also made in one piece. The steel drum casings that unite the two radiators are accurately fitted to the flanges of the castings; and, to insure perfect security, these flanges are sealed up with asbestos cement.

Adaptability.

EITHER hard or soft coal or coke can be employed with satisfaction in the PARAGON FURNACE. No furnace now on the market can more successfully meet the varied requirements of different sections.

42

Hints About Heating.

Superior Durability.

EVERY part of the PARAGON FURNACE is skilfully proportioned in thickness to the amount of strain that it is required to endure. Not only is the PARAGON heavier than other furnaces, but the extra weight of metal is placed *where it will do the most good*. The steel drums are *extra heavy*, with double riveted seams. The fire pot and the lower radiator are *corrugated* throughout. This formation not only largely increases the radiating surface, but also reduces to a minimum the risk of cracking by fire.

In these, as in all other respects, a careful comparison of the PARAGON with all other furnaces is invited. The PARAGON is *no imitation of previous structures*; but in *merit* as in *originality*, it *leads them all*.

PARAGON
STEEL PLATE FURNACES
OCTAGON BASE
WITH EQUALIZED DRAFT

Patented August 5, 1890.

This style is made in three sizes, arranged with different patterns of grates and fire pots, which are distinguished as follows:

Style A.—With Straight Cylinder and " Saxon " Grate.
Style B.—With Straight Cylinder and Triplex Grate.
Style C.—With Curved Cylinder and Frictionless Draw Centre Grate.

Styles A and C have Lever Shakers.

The various cylinders or fire pots used, are so formed as to give the best results with the particular grates for which they are designed.

While the grates of *Styles A and B* demand the use of a cylinder *somewhat larger* at the bottom than at the top, the Draw Centre Grate, used in Style C, which is designed to discharge clinker and refuse at the *centre of the fire*, demands a cylinder *slightly contracted at the bottom*, in order to support the mass of fuel while the fire is being cleaned by the poker.

The use of a cylinder that is expanded outwards at the bottom, with this form of grate, would occasion a risk of dumping a quantity of good coal when cleaning the grate, thereby causing a waste of fuel. Furnaces that employ a fire pot larger at the bottom than at the top, *in connection with a Draw Centre Grate*, are open to serious objections upon this ground.

SHEPPARD'S
STOVES RANGES
AND
FURNACES

Paragon Steel Plate Furnaces.

With Octagon Base. ✳ **Three Sizes.**

Patented August 5, 1890.

Size 32.—Diameter Lower Casing, 32 inches.
Size 36.—Diameter Lower Casing, 36 inches.
Size 40.—Diameter Lower Casing, 40 inches.

PARAGON

STEEL PLATE FURNACES

ROUND BASE

WITH EQUALIZED DRAFT

Patented August 5, 1890.

This style is made in six sizes, all arranged with Curved Cylinder and Draw Centre Grate. All sizes are provided with improved lever shakers. The grate is mounted upon frictionless bearings, and moves so easily that it can be operated by a child. When the clinker doors are opened, the entire lower portion of the fire is exposed to view ; and the poker may be moved freely, at pleasure, over the whole surface of the grate. This is especially desirable if there is any tendency in the coal used to form clinker, or if it is desired to employ soft coal as fuel.

The connecting bar, between the grate shank and the lever shaker, also serves as a handle by which to pull out the centre draw of the grate. This arrangement is exceedingly convenient, and is found only in the furnaces of our manufacture.

The Round Base is extremely pleasing in appearance ; and, while it is very strong and substantial, it is so compact in form as to be less expensive to manufacture, and therefore somewhat lower in price than the Octagon Base.

46

SHEPPARD'S STOVES, RANGES FURNACES.

Paragon Steel Plate Furnaces.

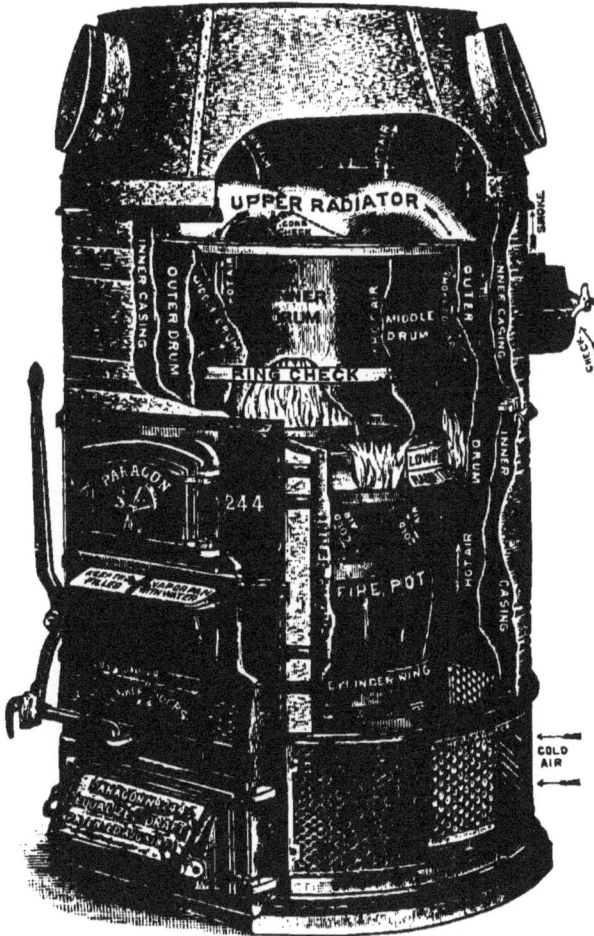

With Round Base.

Six Sizes.

UPPER RADIATOR

INNER CASING

OUTER DRUM

OUTER CASING

MIDDLE DRUM

RING CHECK

INNER DRUM

HOT AIR

INNER CASING

PARAGON

244

FIRE POT

CYLINDER WING

CHECK

SMOKE

COLD AIR

Patented August 5, 1890.

Size 228—Diameter Casing, 28 in.	Size 240—Diameter Casing, 40 in
" 233, " " 33 "	" 244, " " 44 "
" 236, " " 36 "	" 248, " " 48 "

47

Heating Capacity of Paragon Steel Plate Furnaces,

Under Average Conditions. Table A.

Size of Furnace	Heating Capacity In Cubic Feet When Divided into Rooms As in Residences	Heating Capacity In Cubic Feet Undivided As in Churches and Stores	Capacity Sufficient to Employ Hot Air Pipes Of Sizes Below ──OR THEIR EQUIVALENTS──	Cold Air Duct To be Employed Of Size Below ──OR THEIR EQUIVALENTS──	Size of Coal Recommended
No. 32 Paragon	15,000 to 20,000	20,000 to 25,000	4—10 inch	13 x 18 ins.	Medium Stove
" 36 "	18,000 to 25,000	25,000 to 30,000	5—10 "	14 x 20 "	Medium Stove
" 40 "	25,000 to 35,000	35,000 to 45,000	4—12 "	16 x 21 "	L. Stove or Egg
" 228 "	12,000 to 16,000	15,000 to 18,000	4—9 "	12 x 16 "	Medium Stove
" 233 "	15,000 to 20,000	20,000 to 25,000	4—10 "	13 x 18 "	Medium Stove
" 236 "	18,000 to 25,000	25,000 to 30,000	5—10 "	14 x 20 "	Medium Stove
" 240 "	25,000 to 35,000	35,000 to 45,000	4—12 "	16 x 21 "	L. Stove or Egg
" 244 "	30,000 to 40,000	45,000 to 60,000	6—12 "	20 x 25 "	Egg
" 248 "	35,000 to 50,000	60,000 to 80,000	5—14 "	22 x 26 "	Egg

The cold air duct should be of full size indicated until it reaches the furnace, where, if it does not enter a pit beneath the furnace, it should be divided into two branches, each the full size of the cold air opening in the base of the furnace, and so carried around to each side of the furnace.

NOTE.—While under average conditions, if the furnaces are properly set and judiciously managed, these estimates will be found to approximate closely to correctness, yet the exposures of buildings vary so greatly that another table, designated as Table C, which will be found on page 62, has been prepared, whereby the size of furnace that is best suited

SHEPPARD'S STOVES, RANGES, FURNACES

Measurements of Casings, etc., for Paragon Steel Plate Furnaces.

Measures of Circumferences are neat, and do not include lap for seaming or riveting. The Swedging of Lower Galvanized Casing should stop 2 inches from each end, to finish against Furnace Front.

		Lower Galvanized Casing	Upper Galvanized Casing	Lower Inside Casing	Upper Inside Casing	Height of Furnace Uncased	Height of Furnace Finished	Fire Pot Diameter In.	Depth of Fire In.	Size of Smoke Pipe In.
No. 32	Gauge of Sheet Iron	27	27	27	27					
	Height	24 in.	16½ in.	24 in.	16 in.	4 ft. 8¼ in.	5 ft. 6¾ in.	18⅞	15	6
	Circumference	8 ft. 4½ in.	8 ft. 11 in.	6 ft. 5 in.	8 ft. 4¼ in.					
No. 36	Gauge of Sheet Iron	24	24	24	24					
	Height	24 in.	16½ in.	24 in.	16 in.	4 ft. 9 in.	5 ft. 6¾ in.	20¾	15	6
	Circumference	9 ft. 5 in.	9 ft. 11¾ in.	7 ft. 2½ in.	9 ft. 5 in.					
No. 40	Gauge of Sheet Iron	24	24	24	24					
	Height	24 in.	17 in.	24 in.	16½ in.	4 ft. 10¾ in.	5 ft. 8 in.	22¼	15	7
	Circumference	10 ft. 5½ in.	11 ft. ½ in.	7 ft. 11 in.	10 ft. 5½ in.					
No. 228	Gauge of Sheet Iron	27	27	27	27					
	Height	21 in.	15½ in.	21 in.	16½ in.	4 ft. 6 in.	5 ft. 5 in.	15¾	14½	6
	Circumference	7 ft. 3¾ in.	7 ft. 3¾ in.	5 ft. 8 in.	6 ft. 9¾ in.					
No. 233	Gauge of Sheet Iron	27	27	27	27					
	Height	24 in.	15 in.	24 in.	15 in.	4 ft. 8 in.	5 ft. 8 in.	18⅞	15	7
	Circumference	8 ft. 7⅞ in.	8 ft. 7⅞ in.	6 ft. 11 in.	8 ft. ⅞ in.					
No. 236	Gauge of Sheet Iron	24	24	24	24					
	Height	24 in.	15 in.	24 in.	15 in.	4 ft. 10 in.	5 ft. 8¾ in.	20¾	15	7
	Circumference	9 ft. 5 in.	9 ft. 5 in.	7 ft. 8¾ in.	8 ft. 10¾ in.					
No. 240	Gauge of Sheet Iron	24	24	24	24					
	Height	24 in.	15 in.	24 in.	15 in.	5 ft.	5 ft. 9 in.	22½	15½	7
	Circumference	10 ft. 5½ in.	10 ft. 5½ in.	8 ft. 6 in.	9 ft. 11 in.					
No. 244	Gauge of Sheet Iron	24	24	24	21					
	Height	24 in.	14¾	24 in.	14¾ in.	5 ft. ¼ in.	5 ft. 11¾ in.	24⅝	15½	8
	Circumference	10 ft. ⅞ in.	11 ft. 5¾ in.	9 ft. 5¾ in.	10 ft. 10¾ in.					

Hints About Heating.

Directions for Setting the Paragon Furnace
With Octagon Base.

If furnace is to stand over a pit, carry up a central pier of brick work under ash pit, to support weight of furnace. If it is to stand on cellar floor, place under it a course of brick carefully leveled and cemented on top, to prevent dust arising from floor of cellar. Have the furnace base *perfectly level* Place fire pot on ash pit ring, so that notches in fire pot cover projections on ring. Fill in around bottom of fire pot with asbestos cement, a can of which accompanies each furnace. Put dust damper in place, and put the lower dust pipe on the oval collar. Then lift the entire drum section up on fire pot. Secure the upper dust pipe with bolts to oval collar under neck of furnace, and set the drum section in place, with the notches in lower radiator covering the lugs on the fire pot, slipping the upper dust pipe over the lower one. Fill up joint between fire pot and upper radiator with asbestos cement.

Then put on lower galvanized casing, and draw it up neatly to place, bolting it fast to front. Put on the lower inside casing and next fix the lower casing ring (with two flanges on top) in position. Next put on the upper inside casing, taking care to see that the hole in casing around smoke collar is large enough to allow for *free expansion* Then put the upper galvanized casing neatly into place, and then the upper casing ring. Bolt on the draft check and also the upper front. Have all joints properly cemented. Put on the dome top with outlets, and the furnace will be ready to connect with the hot air pipes.

Hints About Heating.

Directions for Setting the Paragon Furnace
With Round Base.

THE furnace base having been carefully placed and leveled up, as in the case of the Octagon Base Furnace, see that the ash pit ring, on sizes No. 244 and No. 248, is in place, with the *lug in front*. On sizes below No. 240, this ring is bolted fast. Cement this ring thoroughly, and then set fire pot in place. Fill in around bottom of fire pot with asbestos cement or sand packing. Complete the setting as directed for the Octagon Base Furnace.

51

Hints About Heating.

Directions for Using Paragon Steel Plate Furnaces.

UNDER the heading "Furnace Management," on page 31, will be found some general comments that will be of service to any one who has charge of a hot air furnace. Some specific directions, applicable to the "PARAGON FURNACE," may also be useful.

To Kindle the Fire.

HAVE the pipe and chimney unobstructed, the grate in its proper position, and the ash pit free from ashes and refuse. Cover the grate well with shavings and small chips. Have a good supply of larger wood ready. Before lighting fire, close check draft at back of furnace, and lift the shutter in ash pit door as far as the ratchet will permit. As soon as the shavings and chips are well kindled, put in the larger wood, a few pieces at a time, until there is a good fire. Put on not more than three or four shovelsful of coal at first. When this is fully ignited, add as many more. After this second supply has been thoroughly kindled, fill up the fire pot, and close the shutter in ash pit door. The check draft at the back must not be opened until all the gas from the fresh coal has passed off. Then, if desired, the fire may be checked enough to keep it burning moderately, although steadily. The feed door should always be kept closed, except when putting on fuel.

Hints About Heating.

To Clear the Fire.

Do not attempt to clear a *low fire*. Let it first burn up for fifteen or twenty minutes. If the furnace be the Round Base Paragon, lift the connecting bar out of the lever shaker, and pull out the centre draw of the grate. Pull out the dust damper, and open the clinker doors. Then with a long poker push all ashes and clinker gently through the central opening of grate. If this is properly done, the whole mass of fuel in the fire pot will remain undisturbed, until the poker has passed over the entire surface of grate. Then push in the centre draw and put the connecting bar into its place. Agitate the lever shaker, and the whole contents of fire pot will settle down, with a clear fire, on the grate. Then push in the dust damper, which must never be out, except when clearing the fire or removing ashes.

If the furnace be the Octagon Base, Style C, the lever shaker must first be thrown as far as possible *to the left*, in order to admit the poker, and the centre draw pulled out with the hooked handle that accompanies the furnace.

The grate of the Octagon Base, Style A, is cleared principally by agitation with the lever shaker, and the fire is dumped by inserting handle into grate shank and turning it over to the left. Clinker may be removed through the poke hole in front of cylinder.

To clear the fire of Style B, with Triplex Grate, or to dump the contents of fire pot, it is only necessary to put the handle perpendicularly on grate shank, and turn it quickly to the *right* until the arrow on handle points *perpendicularly down*. *Remove* the handle, and *replace* it, to repeat the operation, which may be done as often as necessary.

FIDELITY

STEEL PLATE FURNACES

WITH CENTRAL DRAFT

Patented August 5, 1890.   Patented February 16, 1892.

ALTHOUGH the PARAGON FURNACE is the only Three Drum Furnace that can rightfully claim to possess the best possible construction, yet there is a large demand for a three drum furnace of a cheaper form, which shall combine the three requisites of efficiency, durability, and freedom from gas and dust. In the FIDELITY FURNACE these requirements are satisfactorily met, at a moderate cost.

The ash pit is large and strong, amply supporting the weight of the parts above it. The grate is the popular draw centre grate, operated by a lever shaker. A convenient dust flue is provided for the comfort of the operator when removing ashes. The cylinders are very heavy, and their strength, as well as their radiating surface, is greatly increased by corrugation. An ample sand joint between the two cylinders, and one also between the upper cylinder and the bottom drum plate, prevent leakage of gas.

The bottom drum plate has three flanges, and so has also the top radiator, which is made *in one piece*, just as in

Hints About Heating.

the PARAGON FURNACE. The three steel drum casings fit tightly over these flanges, the joints being further secured against leakage of gas by a strong furnace cement. The inner and outer smoke chambers are connected by three channels cast in the top radiator; and above the level of the smoke collar is interposed a self-cleaning ring check, similar to that in the PARAGON FURNACE.

The course of the draft is central, rising through the inner smoke chamber, passing thence through the channels in top radiator to the outer smoke chamber, where its heat is effectively distributed over the whole surface of the drum casings by the action of the graduated ring check.

Every part of the drum casings is strongly heated; and the radiating surface is larger than in any other furnace of same size outer casing known to us, except the PARAGON. The outer drum is cleaned by means of a revolving scraper, upon which a patent has recently been granted. Easy access to this scraper is obtained by simply opening the clean out door shown in the cut. By drawing out the clean out slide, just over feed door, an opening is made from the outer drum into the neck of the furnace, through which all soot and ashes drop as soon as the scraper is revolved.

The clean out door is provided with a register, which makes an excellent check draft, enabling the operator perfectly to control the process of combustion.

The construction of the FIDELITY FURNACES is such as to admit of the cold air supply being taken directly from the cellar, or from outside the house by means of a cold air duct. The latter method is, of course, always to be preferred.

55

FIDELITY

STEEL PLATE FURNACES

WITH CENTRAL DRAFT

Patented August 5, 1890.   Patented February 16, 1892.

IN style, finish and durability, we unhesitatingly affirm that these goods have no superior at the same price, while in efficiency they are surpassed only by the PARAGON FURNACES.

The bottom of the FIDELITY FURNACE is open, permitting the cold air supply to be taken from a pit beneath the furnace if desired ; or the furnace may be placed upon feet and front support, as shown in the cut, and the cold air taken from the cellar. By removing the feet and front support, placing the furnace directly upon the cellar floor, and using a cold air collar on the back of the lower casing, direct connection may be made with a cold air duct at the back of the furnace.

The lever shaker and connecting bar, with the draw centre grate, are arranged precisely as in the ROUND BASE PARAGON. The clinker door is large and gives easy access with the poker to every part of the grate surface. The grate can easily be removed and replaced through the ash pit door at any time, when necessary. The drums are made of heavy steel plate, double riveted. The whole construction is such as to secure a high degree of efficiency and durability at a moderate price ; and where the large capacity and the special features of the PARAGON are not required, the FIDELITY FURNACE may be selected with entire confidence in its desirability.

Fidelity Steel Plate Furnaces.

THREE SIZES.

Patented August 5, 1890, and February 16, 1892.

No. 24.—Diameter Casing, 24 inches.

No. 28.—Diameter Casing, 28 inches.

No. 32.—Diameter Casing, 32 inches.

Heating Capacity of Fidelity Steel Plate Furnaces,

Under Average Conditions. Table B.

Size of Furnace	Heating Capacity In Cubic Feet When Divided into Rooms As in Residences	Heating Capacity In Cubic Feet Undivided As in Churches and Stores	Capacity Sufficient to Employ Hot Air Pipes Of Sizes Below ⌐OR THEIR EQUIVALENTS⌐	Cold Air Duct To be Employed Of Size Below ⌐OR THEIR EQUIVALENTS⌐	Size of Coal Recommended
No. 24 Fidelity	5,000 to 8,000	6,000 to 9,000	Three 8 inch	8 x 13 ins.	Small Stove
" 28 "	7,000 to 10,000	10,000 to 12,000	Three 9 inch	9 x 16 ins.	Medium Stove
" 32 "	9,000 to 13,000	12,000 to 15,000	Three 10 inch	10 x 18 ins.	Medium Stove

NOTE.—While under average conditions, if the furnaces are properly set and judiciously managed, these estimates will be found to approximate closely to correctness, yet the exposures of buildings vary so greatly that another table, designated as Table C, which will be found on page 62, has been prepared, whereby the size of furnace that is best suited to any given case may be more accurately determined.

Hints About Heating.

Measurements of Casings, etc., for Fidelity Steel Plate Furnaces.

Measures of Circumferences are neat, and do not include lap for seaming or riveting. The Swedging of Lower Galvanized Casing should stop 2 inches from each end, to finish against Furnace Front.	Lower Galvanized Casing	Upper Galvanized Casing	Inside Casing
No. 24 Gauge of Sheet Iron..	27	27	27
Height.............	16 ins.	24 ins.	24 ins.
Circumference.......	6 ft. 3¼ ins.	6 ft. 3¼ ins.	4 ft. 6 ins.
No. 28 Gauge of Sheet Iron..	27	27	27
Height	16½ ins.	24 ins.	24 ins.
Circumference.......	7 ft. 3¾ ins.	7 ft. 3¾ ins.	5 ft. 5 ins.
No. 32 Gauge of Sheet Iron..	27	27	27
Height.............	17¾ ins.	24 ins.	24 ins.
Circumference.......	8 ft. 4½ ins.	8 ft. 4½ ins.	6 ft. 3½ ins.

HEIGHT OF FURNACE INCLUDES FEET	Height of Furnace Uncased	Height of Furnace Finished	Fire Pot Diameter In.	Depth of Fire In.	Size of Smoke Pipe In.
No. 24 Fidelity.............	4 ft. 7 in.	5 ft. ½ in.	13¼	11½	6
" 28 "	4 ft. 7½ in.	5 ft. ½ in.	15¾	11¾	6
" 32 "	4 ft. 10 in.	5 ft. 2½ ins.	17¾	12½	7

Hints About Heating.

Directions for Setting Fidelity Steel Plate Furnaces.

If the cold air is to be taken from a pit beneath the furnace, let a central pier be carried up under ash pit to support the weight of furnace. Otherwise, have a good brick or cement floor under furnace, and see that the furnace stands firmly on the feet; or, if not using feet, let the base rim rest solidly upon the floor, the furnace base in all instances to be perfectly level.

Place fire pot in position, carefully cementing it around the bottom with asbestos cement, or making a good sand joint. Put in the dust damper, and place the lower dust pipe on oval collar, and bolt fast to ash pit top. Bolt the upper dust pipe to collar on neck of upper cylinder, and slip it over the lower pipe, bringing the upper cylinder to its proper position upon the fire pot, and carefully cementing the joint between them.

Carefully place in position the lower galvanized casing and put on the lower casing ring. Then put the inside casing into its place. Cement the grooves on the top of the upper cylinder and neck, and then lift the drum section to its place and bolt it down. Then put on the upper galvanized casing and the top casing ring. Bolt the feed door frame in position, and then the check door frame, cementing all crevices. Bolt on the smoke collar, and put on the dome top with hot air outlets. The furnace will then be ready to connect with the hot air pipes. It is well to cover the dome top to a level with fine sand to diminish the radiation of heat from the top of furnace.

·Hints About Heating·

Directions for Using Fidelity Steel Plate Furnaces.

To Kindle the Fire.

THE check draft of the FIDELITY FURNACE is at the front, over the feed door, and not at the back as in the PARAGON. Before lighting fire close this check draft, and also the feed door, and open the ash pit door. In other particulars, proceed as directed in the case of the PARAGON FURNACE, on page 52. A direct draft may be obtained, if desired, by drawing out the sliding damper over feed door.

To Clear the Fire.

THE directions given in the case of the ROUND BASE PARAGON, on page 53, apply without change to the FIDELITY FURNACE.

To Clean the Outer Drum.

THE inner drum is self cleaning. To clean the outer drum, close feed door and pull out the sliding damper above it. Open the clean out door, and insert the hand through it. Take hold of the revolving scraper and pull it around three or four times, and all soot and ashes in the drum will fall into the furnace neck, and thence through dust flue into the ash pit.

To Check the Fire.

CLOSE register wheels in ash pit door and open the check draft register in clean out door. If this does not moderate the fire sufficiently, the clean out door itself may be placed ajar as much as may be necessary to effect the desired result.

Index of Heating Capacities. Table C.

FOR INSTRUCTIONS, SEE PAGE 63.

| FIDELITY FURNACES | | | PARAGON STEEL PLATE FURNACES | | | | | | | | |
| | | | OCTAGON BASE | | | ROUND BASE | | | | | |
No. 24	No. 28	No. 32	No. 32	No. 36	No. 40	No. 228	No. 233	No. 236	No. 240	No. 244	No. 248
15	22	28	35	44	52	32	39	46	53	63	74
16	23	29	36	45	53	33	40	47	54	64	75
17	24	30	37	46	54	34	41	48	55	65	76
18	25	31	38	47	55	35	42	49	56	66	77
19	26	32	39	48	56	36	43	50	57	67	78
20	27	33	40	49	57	37	44	51	58	68	79
21	28	34	41	50	58	38	45	52	59	69	80
22	29	35	42	51	59	39	46	53	60	70	81
23	..	36	43	52	60	40	47	54	61	71	82
24	..	37	44	53	61	41	48	55	62	72	83
..	..	..	45	54	62	42	49	56	63	73	84
..	..	..	46	55	63	..	..	..	64	74	85
..	..	..	47	56	64	..	..	..	65	75	86
..	..	..	..	..	65	..	..	..	..	76	87
..	..	..	..	..	..	..	..	..	..	77	88

Hints About Heating.

Instructions for Use of "Table C."

To find size of furnace or furnaces best adapted to any building, ascertain the contents of building in cubic feet, the number of square feet of exposed wall surface, and the number of square feet of glass in windows. Then calculate by the following rule:

RULE—1. Multiply the cubic feet of contents by $8/10$, the square feet of exposed wall by 4, and the square feet of glass by 40, and add together the several products.

2. Divide the sum by **600**, if the space in building is divided into rooms as in a residence; or by **800** if the space is undivided, as in a church or store.

3. Look in **Table C** for the quotient thus arrived at. The furnace indicated in the column in which such number is found, is the furnace to be recommended for the building in question.

NOTE.—If the quotient number be found in *more than one column*, it indicates that either furnace indicated will do the work. The larger of the two is, however, to be preferred, as being the more durable.

NOTE.—If the quotient number be *higher* than the highest number in **Table C**, *two* or *more* furnaces will be required, of such sizes as are indicated by the *highest component numbers* of the quotient number that appear in the Table.

EXAMPLES—1. A residence has 9,500 cubic feet of space, 620 square feet exposed wall and 180 square feet glass. Find suitable furnace.

$$9,500 \times 8/10 = 7,600$$
$$620 \times 4 = 2,480$$
$$180 \times 40 = 7,200$$

Quotient
$$17,280 \div 600 = 28 +$$

In **Table C**, the quotient number **28** is found both in column headed "No. 28" and also in that headed "No. 32 **Fidelity Furnace**." This indicates that while "No. 28" will do the work, "No. 32" is preferable.

Instructions for Use of "Table C," Continued.

2. A residence has 31,200 cubic feet of space, 1,425 square feet exposed wall, and 340 square feet glass. Find suitable furnace or furnaces.

$$31,200 \times {}^8/_{10} = 24,960$$
$$1,425 \times 4 = 5,700$$
$$340 \times 40 = 13,600$$

Quotient
$$44,260 \div 600 = 73 +$$

The quotient number appears in column headed "**No. 244 Paragon Furnace.**" The component numbers **33** and **40**, the sum of which equals **73**, appear in columns headed respectively "**No. 228**" and "**No. 233 Paragon Furnace.**" Therefore you may use either one "**No. 244**," or, if two furnaces can be more conveniently used, one "**No. 228**" and also one "**No. 233 Paragon**" instead.

3. A church has 143,000 cubic feet space, 5,600 square feet exposed wall, and 1,150 square feet glass. Find suitable furnaces.

$$143,000 \times {}^8/_{10} = 114,400$$
$$5,600 \times 4 = 22,400$$
$$1,150 \times 40 = 46,000$$

Quotient
$$182,800 \div 800 = 228 +$$

The quotient is higher than appears in Table. The component number **57** appears in column headed "**No. 240 Paragon**," ($57 \times 4 = 228$). So that *four* "**No. 240 Paragons**" will do the work. The component number **76** appears in columns headed "**No. 244 and No. 248 Paragon**" ($76 \times 3 = 228$). Hence *three* "**No. 244**," or, preferably, three "**No. 248 Paragons**" may be employed.

Model of Paragon Furnace.

A nickel plated model, 8 inches in diameter of base, and complete in all its parts, will be sent to any architect or builder, on receipt of $2.50, and the expressage will be prepaid to any place in the New England, Middle or Southern Atlantic States. Should its examination result in the purchase of a furnace, the amount paid for the model will be credited on the bill; or it will be refunded to any one who shall return the model in good order, with express charges paid.

www.ingramcontent.com/pod-product-compliance
Lightning Source LLC
Chambersburg PA
CBHW021629270326
41931CB00008B/939